Lizzie Learns About Lying

Written by Gary Hogg • Illustrated by Gary R. Anderson

ISBN 0-930771-08-7—Soft Bound

Little Buckaroo Books

Printed August 2010 in the USA   10 9 8 7 6 5 4 3 2 1

Open your eyes and look as far as you can,
One look farther, there lies a very strange land.

A land where everyone loves to tell lies.
All the folks there are liars, yes, even the flies.
Right next to a rock near the big waterfall
Lived Lizzie the lizard, the worst liar of all.

She'd tell snakes their behinds were in knots.
She'd tell leopards they had lost all their spots.

She'd tell turtles they had holes in their shells.
There was no end to the lies Lizzie would tell.

One day Lizzie changed the maps and the signs.
She changed the arrows and she changed the lines.
If a sign said "stop," Lizzie made it say "go."
If a sign said "yes," she changed it to "no."
Lizzie didn't care. She thought it was fun.
She didn't see how it could hurt anyone.

The Happy Hawk, who was soaring high overhead,
Made a wrong turn because of a sign that he read.
The sign said to "criss," but it should have said "cross."
The Hawk circled and circled until he was lost.

Finally, he landed near the big waterfall.
He'd barely sat down when he heard a loud call.

"Help me! Help me! I think I am dying.
Help me! Help me!" Someone kept crying.
He jumped to his feet like a life-saving hawk,
And ran straight to the commotion behind the rock.

There he found Lizzie telling lie after lie.
"Why are you lying?" he asked. "Why lizard, why?"
Lizzie saw that the Hawk was a very mad bird
But she didn't stop. She said more lying words.

"Before you accuse me of being a liar,
You'd better cool off. Your cape is on fire!"

"Oh no," yelled the Hawk. "I don't want to bake!
Oh no," yelled the Hawk and he jumped in the lake.

He splashed and he thrashed for a minute or two,
Until he saw Lizzie laughing herself blue.

He leaped from the lake before Lizzie could flee.
"You silly reptile, why do you always lie to me?

You just gave me a scare and made me get wet.
You're the biggest liar that I've ever met.

You like to tell lies. You think that it's fun.
You think that your lying won't hurt anyone.

You are the one who will get hurt in the end.
Sooner or later you won't have any friends.

We all need friends to help us get by
But a friend doesn't want to be told a lie."

The Happy Hawk then took off in flight
Hoping that Lizzie would change for the right.

The rest of the liars were in for a shock
When Lizzie followed the advice of the Hawk.
She said she was sorry for her dishonest ways.
She said she'd be truthful the rest of her days.

She then talked to the snakes, turtles and flies.
She talked everyone into not telling lies.

Lizzie's now happy and so are her friends.
They all tell the truth from beginning to end.